Consultant Neville Linton
Managing Editor Belinda Hollyer
Editor Kate Woodhouse
Design Jerry Watkiss
Picture Research Caroline Mitchell
Production Rosemary Bishop
Illustrations Raymond Turvey
Hayward Art Group
Maps Matthews & Taylor Associates
Author's assistants Sandra Bethell
Rudolph Eastman
Judy Khan

Page 6: Fishing off Carriacou, the largest of the Grenadines

Contents page: The Carenage, St Georges, Grenada

Agency for Public Information, Jamaica: 39B, All-Sport: 25TL, Mike Andrews: 31BL, BBC Hulton Picture Library: 14B, 15T, Bodleian Library: 26BR, Bo Bojesen: 35TL, 36BL, 38T, 39TR, Anne Bolt: Cover BL, 20T, 21TR, 30T & B, 41T, Camera Press: 24T, 26T, 27TR & BR, 29BR, 33BR, 37BL, Caribbean Chronicle: 23BR, Bruce Coleman Limited : 9B, 22L, Coconut Industry Board: 29BL, Colorific: 25TL, Compix: Cover BR, 9C, 28B, 31TL, 36R, 37TL, Mary Evans Picture Library: 15B, Explorer: 33BL, Format/Jenny Matthews: Cover TR, John Griffiths: 37TR, Susan Griggs Agency: 11B, Robert Harding Picture Library: Cover T, endpapers, 10T, 11TL, 29TR, 39TL, Richard Hart: 20B, John & Penny Hubley: 19L, 32–33, 39BR, Alan Hutchison Library: 6–7, 10–11, 11TR, 19R, 34T, 41B, Jamaican Tourist Board: 22B, 23TL, 24B, William MacQuitty: 25TR, 33T, 34B, 35TR, Macdonald Library: 12BR, 16B, 37BR, Macdonald Library/Barnes & Webster: 35B, Mansell Collection: 17B, National Maritime Museum: 12T, 12BL, 14R, New Beacon Books: 21TL, Network/Mike Abrahams: 32B, Osiris Films: 22T, Photosource: 26BL, Popperfoto: 21B, Rex Features: 9TL, 27BL, Royal Commonwealth Society: 18T, Spectrum Colour Library: 8T, 31BR, Homer Sykes: 38B, John Topham Picture Library: 8B, Mireille Vautier: 17T, 23BL, 24BL, Zefa: Cover TL, 9TR, 23R, 24BR, 28T, 29TL, 31TR.

A MACDONALD BOOK
© Macdonald & Co (Publishers) Ltd 1980, 1987

First published in Great Britain in 1980 by Macdonald & Co (Publishers) Ltd London & Sydney
A BPCC plc company

Printed in Great Britain by Purnell Book Production Ltd Member of the BPCC Group

Macdonald & Co (Publishers) Ltd
Greater London House
Hampstead Road
London NW1 7QX

British Library Cataloguing in Publication Data
Springer, Eintou Pearl
The Caribbean.—2nd ed.—(Countries new edition)
1. Caribbean area—Social life and customs
I. Title   II. Campbell, Ken, 1928–. Caribbean   III. Series
909'.09821   F2169

ISBN 0-356-11812-6
ISBN 0-356-11813-4 Pbk

The Caribbean

the lands and their peoples

Eintou Pearl Springer

Macdonald Educational

Contents

Sea of contrasts

The Caribbean is the name given to a group of countries in and around the Caribbean Sea. The islands of the region stretch for 3600km from Florida in North America to Venezuela in South America. The four mainland Caribbean countries are Belize, French Guiana, Guyana and Surinam. They are in Central and South America.

The Caribbean countries share a common history. They are all countries which were conquered and settled by Europeans in the sixteenth century. Their original populations were mostly destroyed, and their natural resources exploited by the European settlers. Most of the countries were run as sugar plantations using first slaves from Africa and then indentured contract labour to work them. The sugar and other crops were all sent to Europe. All the countries of the Caribbean were colonies of Europe. Today only a few remain as dependencies, notably Anguilla, the British Virgin Islands and the Turks and Caicos Islands.

The name Caribbean comes from one of the Amerindian peoples who first inhabited the islands: the Caribs. Christopher Columbus called the islands the West Indies because he thought he had reached India when he sailed west from Europe on his voyages of exploration.

Natural features and climate
The Caribbean is an area of great variety and contrast – in its landscape, its peoples, its wildlife and vegetation and its natural resources. The flatness of Barbados or Curaçao is very different from the hills and valleys of Grenada, Trinidad or St Vincent and different again from the mountains of Guyana or Haiti. The inner islands from Saba to Grenada are of volcanic origin; some volcanoes like Mt Pelée in Martinique still spit their ash threateningly. The dense forests of Belize contrast with the coral and limestone islands of Anguilla and Barbados.

▲ The beach at Charlotteville, Tobago. The Caribbean scenery is a precious asset, but care is needed to ensure that it is not spoilt by overdevelopment for tourism.

▼ A flock of scarlet ibis taking off. Every evening at sunset waves of these spectacular birds can be seen flying over the Caroni Swamp, just south of Port of Spain in Trinidad.

The climate is tropical, but within this broad definition there are variations. The mountainous and hilly countries tend to have a higher rainfall than the flatter ones. Between June and November the countries from Tobago northwards are in danger of being lashed by the furious winds of hurricanes. Some countries live under the additional threat of earthquakes.

People and wildlife
Equally diverse are the people of the Caribbean. These are mainly the native Amerindians, the descendants of the European settlers, the slaves from Africa and the indentured workers from India and China.

The wildlife of the Caribbean ranges from the huge colonies of flamingoes in the Bahamas and Bonaire to the manatee, an unusual sea mammal found in Guyana and in the South American rivers which flow into the Atlantic. The mountain chicken of Dominica and Montserrat is unique to the area, despite its name it is not a bird but a giant frog. Both tropical and temperate plants grow in the region. The St Vincent botanical gardens, laid out in 1763, have some particularly fine plants. Mahogany from the Dominican Republic is a popular hardwood used for making furniture. In Trinidad there are no fewer than four hundred species of butterfly.

▲ The active volcano Mt Pelée which dominates the island of Martinique. In 1902 the volcano erupted, engulfing all 30,000 inhabitants of St Pierre, the town below it. The town has been rebuilt. The volcano remains active, but quiet.

▲ This scene of destruction in Roseau, Dominica, shows the damage caused by Hurricane David in August 1979. In just a few hours three-quarters of the population of Dominica lost their homes as roofs were ripped off and walls demolished. The hurricane then moved north-westwards where a few days later several hundred people were killed when it devastated parts of the Dominican Republic. In addition most of the banana plantations of Dominica were destroyed.

► The flame tree in Antigua is a fine example of the ravishing flowering plants to be found in the Caribbean. The colours of the trees and flowers are vibrant and bright.

◄ This green turtle has come ashore to lay her eggs. Sea turtles usually spend their life in tropical seas but the females come ashore to lay their eggs. They drag themselves up the beach, dig a pit about 60cm deep and lay a clutch of about a hundred eggs in ten minutes. Then they return to the sea. The eggs hatch seventeen days later, but very few baby turtles reach maturity. Turtles are an endangered species after many years of over-hunting for their shell and flesh. There is now a turtle farm on the Cayman Islands which aims to replenish stocks. Sea turtles' nesting beaches are found on several Caribbean islands, including some in the Bahamas, Barbuda and Guadeloupe.

The Amerindians

Up until the end of the fifteenth century there were about six groups of indigenous peoples living in the Caribbean. They are known, together, as Amerindians. The most important of these groups were the Arawaks and the Caribs.

The Arawaks migrated from the South American mainland from the Orinoco river basin. They left the dense tropical rain forests of the Amazon and crossed the sea to Trinidad. From there they gradually travelled through the islands northwards until they reached the Bahamas. They did not settle permanently in any island until they came to Hispaniola, which is now Haiti and the Dominican Republic, in about AD1000. The Arawaks were skilled farmers and fishermen. They grew tobacco, maize, beans, peanuts and potatoes. They cultivated cassava as their staple food and could manufacture cotton goods. They lived in light, simple shelters of palm leaves. Their descendants still survive in the dense tropical rainforests of Guyana.

The Caribs were the last of the indigenous peoples to come to the Caribbean. Their name comes from Caribal, which means valiant men. They were different from the Arawaks in that they were more war-like. They moved northwards, probably from Bolivia in South America.

By AD1000 they had travelled from the Orinoco basin to the islands of the Caribbean. They swept the Arawaks before them, raiding the settlements. Once they had conquered a settlement the Caribs would take it over and rebuilt it. In this way they settled islands as far north as Puerto Rico. The Arawaks remained undisturbed further north in Hispaniola and the Bahamas. In spite of their enmity the Caribs and the Arawaks had a similar domestic lifestyle. Many Caribbean people claim part of their ancestry as Carib, the valiant people who fought to the death and would not be enslaved by anyone.

Explorers from the east

There is evidence that the first explorers from the east to arrive in the Caribbean could have been the Vikings in their long ships or Africans coming as traders and explorers. In 1492 Christopher Columbus sailed from Spain, thinking he would reach India on a westerly route and instead landed on an island in the Bahamas which he named San Salvador. He found evidence of gold in the Bahamas, Cuba and Hispaniola. When he returned to Spain it was the promise of untold wealth in the West Indies which led the nobility of Spain to finance another three voyages to the Caribbean in search of gold. Columbus was followed by other European explorers and soon the Caribs and Arawaks were the hapless victims of massacres, disease and slavery. Between 1492 and 1496 about two-thirds of the mainly Arawak population of a quarter of a million in Hispaniola had died. By 1548 only five hundred were still alive.

The arrival of the Spanish in the Caribbean completely altered the life of the indigenous peoples. The Spanish craved the wealth the New World seemed to offer and were willing to acquire it at any price, which included killing thousands of Arawaks and Caribs.

▲ The ruins of a Mayan temple at Xunantunich in Belize. The Maya, who lived in Central America, were virtually destroyed by the Spanish. They were treated in much the same way as the Caribs and Arawaks.

 ▲ This Amerindian family living in Guyana are Arawaks. They live a separate life from the rest of the population of Guyana, carrying on the ancient customs and traditions of their ancestors.

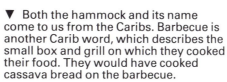 ▼ Both the hammock and its name come to us from the Caribs. Barbecue is another Carib word, which describes the small box and grill on which they cooked their food. They would have cooked cassava bread on the barbecue.

▲ A Carib boy, whose distinctive features show him to be a descendant of one of the original peoples of the Caribbean. Caribs live mainly in Dominica, but mixed descendants also live in St Vincent and Trinidad.

▼ The cathedral of Santo Domingo, capital of the Dominican Republic, houses the tomb of Christopher Columbus. In his voyages of exploration Columbus visited and re-named most of the Caribbean islands.

The European settlers

Spain was very anxious that its newly discovered source of wealth in the West Indies should not be shared with other European countries. The King of Spain sought the Pope's help in claiming the West Indies. In 1494 the Pope signed the Treaty of Tordesillas, which drew an imaginary line through the Atlantic Ocean from north to south. The newly discovered lands to the west of this line were to be exclusively Spanish territory, the lands to the east of the line were to be Portuguese.

It was however impossible for Spain to protect her territories in the Caribbean. Spanish warships, called galleons, patrolled the region attempting to keep out intruders. Any intruders caught were brutally killed. Even so the other Europeans found the attractions of the Caribbean hard to resist: the Spanish treasure ships, the tobacco for which the Europeans had now acquired a taste. In addition, Spain's enemies used conflicts in Europe as an excuse for attacking Spanish possessions in the Caribbean.

Spain's enemies

The Portuguese were the first Europeans to trespass on Spain's newly acquired territory. They traded slaves from their own territories in West Africa and European goods for gold from the West Indies. By 1500 French pirates or 'corsairs' were openly attacking Spanish vessels bound for Europe, seizing the goods aboard and taking them back to France. They also attacked Spanish settlements in Hispaniola.

The English were also keen to exploit the wealth of the West Indies. Francis Drake, Henry Morgan and Edward 'Bluebeard' Teach all grew rich on their plundering of the West Indies and Spanish traders. Although these raids damaged Spanish trade for short periods, Spain was still the most powerful European country in the Caribbean at the end of the sixteenth century.

▲ Edward Teach's hair, plaited with firebrands, must have frightened many Amerindians and Spanish sailors.

▼ This 'piece of eight' was made from gold plundered by the Spanish from the Amerindians. It might once have been an intricately worked ornament, melted down and reused as a coin.

The end of Spanish supremacy
It was the Dutch who broke the Spanish monopoly in the Caribbean. At the beginning of the seventeenth century they started to trade with Venezuela for salt. Their trading then extended to tobacco and other goods from Guyana and then the islands of the West Indies. In 1621 the Dutch West India Company was founded to set up trading stations protected and supported by Dutch ships. In 1629 the Dutch succeeded in capturing an entire Spanish treasure fleet, the greatest loss the Spanish had suffered. This was the final blow to Spanish supremacy in the Caribbean.

The founding of colonies
The English and French began to attack Spanish colonies and to settle new ones in the Eastern Caribbean. In 1625 Sir Thomas Warner founded the first successful British colony of St Christopher, now known as St Kitts. The English and French living together on St Kitts attacked and massacred all the Caribs on the island.

It was private companies which first settled the countries of the Caribbean, but in 1660 the British government took control of those islands which their subjects had colonised, and in 1670 the French government did the same. Although it was the Dutch who broke Spain's domination of the Caribbean, it was the British who eventually became the biggest colonisers in the region.

▼ *Santa Maria*, the ship in which Columbus sailed from Spain to the West Indies. Life on board was hard, especially for the first voyagers who feared that sailing west they would sail off the edge of the world.

▶ ▼ The ownership of Caribbean countries was often changed in treaties concluding European wars. These maps show who owned the Eastern Caribbean islands in 1674 and then in 1764. The map below shows the whole region in 1815. This was the last major change and tends to reflect the language spoken in each country today.

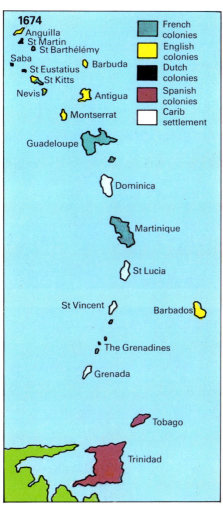

1674

- Anguilla
- St Martin
- St Barthélémy
- Saba
- St Eustatius
- Barbuda
- St Kitts
- Nevis
- Antigua
- Montserrat
- Guadeloupe
- Dominica
- Martinique
- St Lucia
- St Vincent
- Barbados
- The Grenadines
- Grenada
- Tobago
- Trinidad

Legend:
- French colonies
- English colonies
- Dutch colonies
- Spanish colonies
- Carib settlement

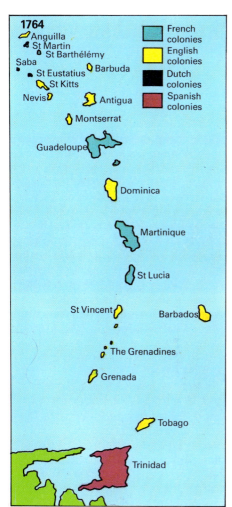

1764

- Anguilla
- St Martin
- St Barthélémy
- Saba
- St Eustatius
- Barbuda
- St Kitts
- Nevis
- Antigua
- Montserrat
- Guadeloupe
- Dominica
- Martinique
- St Lucia
- St Vincent
- Barbados
- The Grenadines
- Grenada
- Tobago
- Trinidad

Legend:
- French colonies
- English colonies
- Dutch colonies
- Spanish colonies

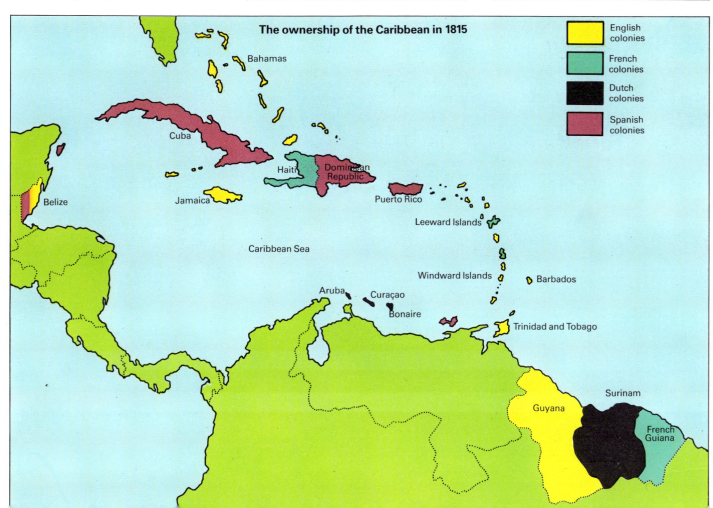

The ownership of the Caribbean in 1815

- Bahamas
- Cuba
- Haiti
- Dominican Republic
- Jamaica
- Belize
- Puerto Rico
- Leeward Islands
- Caribbean Sea
- Windward Islands
- Barbados
- Aruba
- Curaçao
- Bonaire
- Trinidad and Tobago
- Guyana
- Surinam
- French Guiana

Legend:
- English colonies
- French colonies
- Dutch colonies
- Spanish colonies

Sugar and slavery

Sugar completely changed the course of settlement and development in the Caribbean. Up until the seventeenth century tobacco was the main crop for export. It was grown on small-holdings, often worked by only one man. However, by about 1640, tobacco from the American colonies was both better quality and cheaper. At the same time people in Europe were having to pay ever increasing prices for honey, the traditional sweetener. It seemed then that sugar cane, which Columbus had brought from the East on his second voyage in 1494, was the obvious crop to replace tobacco.

Sugar was very expensive to produce. It needed a large initial outlay of money and a large labour force. Labour was needed for the preparation and planting of the cane; repair of equipment and barrel-making; the cutting and transporting of cane to the mills; the processing in the mills, until finally it was ready for shipping to Europe.

Africans as slaves
At first the Europeans attempted to use the Amerindians for this work, but this was not successful. Their numbers had dwindled after many years of mistreatment and those that remained resisted any attempt to enslave them. In 1515 a Spanish priest recommended to the Spanish government that Africans should replace the Amerindian workforce. In 1517 the Portuguese were granted an *asiento* or licence by the Spanish to supply African slaves to the Caribbean. Over the next 350 years about ten million, no one is sure of the exact number, Africans were taken to the New World as slaves.

Slavery was brutal and inhumane. Africans were seized from all along the western coast from what is now Senegal to the Congo. Many did not survive the journey, which could take up to six months. They died from disease, lack of food and excessive beating.

A slave's life
When they arrived in the West Indies the slaves were sold without consideration of family, friendship or tribal links. They became the property of the plantation owner. They could not leave the plantation without written permission; no one was responsible for their welfare. They lived in houses provided by the planters, with a plot of land on which they grew their food. They worked about fifteen hours a day, six days a week and so had little time to tend their plots. The plantation owners allocated them clothes about twice a year. Their main source of protein was imported salted fish.

The slave traders
The Portuguese were the principal slave traders during the sixteenth century. But it was John Hawkins, an Englishman, who built up the infamous triangular trade. Goods, woven cotton or firearms for example, were exported from England to Africa and traded for slaves. The slaves were then transported to the New World on the 'middle passage' and traded for sugar. This was then shipped to England. By the seventeenth century the Dutch controlled the slave trade. Control then passed to the British and later the French.

The slave trade was finally abolished by the British in 1807, the Dutch in 1814, the Spanish in 1829 and the French in 1830. Slavery was not abolished until 1834.

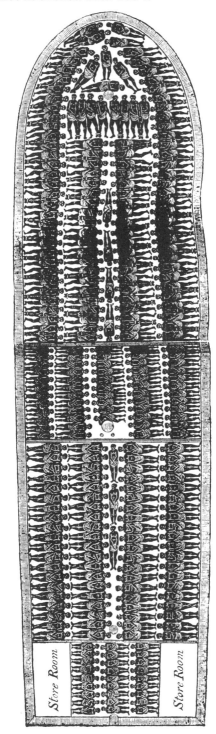

◄ A barracoon or hut (below left), where slaves would be taken after capture. The newly captured Africans would be examined by the ship's surgeon and sorted into the fit and the old or unhealthy. Those who were fit would be branded and kept in the barracoon until the next ship sailed for the New World. Treatment in the barracoons was particularly bad, merchants tried to cut their costs by not feeding the slaves properly.

◄ This picture shows the way in which slaves were transported across the world. The men lay in a place two metres long, 40 centimetres wide and 1 metre high, the women had slightly less space. They were chained together and only allowed out once a day for a short period of exercise. The ship owners wanted to keep the slaves fit for sale, but in these terrible conditions this was not likely.

► Cutting the cane. The tall canes were cut with a machete knife, then each cane was stripped of its leaves and cut into smaller pieces. It was hard and back-breaking work, done by men and women alike.

▼ The cane was then ground, as in this mill. The next stage was to boil the grounds in water until sugar crystals were formed. These were then poured into barrels.

Resistant Africa

Resistance began with the first few slaves who were taken to the Caribbean via Europe. They ran away into the bush and joined the Arawaks. The first slave ship arrived in the Caribbean in 1517; the first revolt was in 1518. From 1518 to 1831 there were at least fifty major slave revolts in the Spanish, Dutch, English and French Caribbean.

The fight against slavery began on the journey to the Caribbean. Many jumped overboard to certain death rather than become a slave, others planned revolts even on the ships. Once on the plantations many slaves ran away, although they knew they risked being flogged, maimed or tortured if they were captured, which they often were.

Free communities

Some slaves managed to avoid capture and set up free communities. The most famous of these were the Maroons of Jamaica and the Djukas of Surinam. The Maroons in Jamaica established their first community in the mountains in 1655, but this only lasted up to 1739. The Djukas settled in the forests and swamps of Surinam. Their descendants still live there and in many different ways continue the traditional crafts and lifestyle. The Maroons of Belize, St Lucia and St Vincent mixed with the Caribs of those countries.

The slave owners did all they could to suppress the African slaves, but the slaves continued to fight back. If they could not escape, they would mutilate or poison themselves so that they could not work. In addition the slaves made every effort to keep their culture alive. Their songs and stories gave them hope and comfort and sometimes an opportunity to mock their masters. The stories of Anansi, the clever spider, were particularly important in this. The slave owners tried to weaken them by buying slaves from different tribes, so that they would not speak the same language and therefore could not plot against their masters.

The slave system survived because of the huge profits it brought to the plantation owners. However, by the beginning of the nineteenth century slavery was under threat. The abolition of the slave trade meant the end of the supply of free labour, and the reduction of the market for sugar because of the wars in Europe meant that the price of sugar became very high.

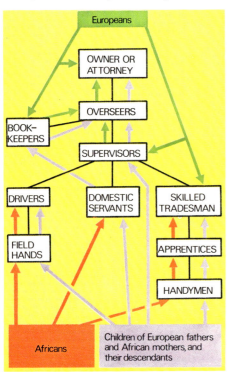

The social structure of a Caribbean plantation. Europeans were in charge while Africans did the menial work. Even after slavery was abolished the pattern did not change very much for many years.

Fanti Tiwi name	Jamaican name
Kwabena	Cubina
Kwaku	Quaco
Kofi	Cuffee
Kwamina/Kwami	Quamina
Kwaku	Quamin
Kodwo	Cudjoe

▲ Jamaican names and their equivalent in the Fanti language of Ghana. Slaves were forbidden to use their own names and had to take a nickname or the name of their master. Some people nevertheless managed to preserve the old names and today they are becoming more popular again.

▼ A statue of Paul Bogle, leader of the Morant Bay rebellion in Jamaica. In the reprisals which followed Bogle was executed by the colonial authorities.

The first black republic

In 1804 the first black republic in the New World was proclaimed. The slaves of the French colony of St Domingue were among the worst-treated in the Caribbean. They revolted against their masters under the leadership of Toussaint in 1791 and Dessalines in 1804 fighting off both the British and the French. They restored the country's original Arawak name Haiti, which means 'the high place'.

At the same time the anti-slavery movement in Europe was formed stressing the immorality of slavery. These four factors combined to force an end to slavery. Slavery was abolished in the British colonies in 1834, the French in 1848, the Dutch in 1852 and the Spanish in 1886.

The freeing or emancipation of the slaves did not mean the end of African resistance. The slave owners received huge compensation for the loss of their slaves from their home government, but the slaves received nothing. In 1865 there was a rebellion by former slaves at Morant Bay in Jamaica demanding more land for themselves. This rebellion was brutally suppressed, 600 people were executed, 600 were flogged and a thousand homes were destroyed.

▲ A painting in the Haitian style showing Toussaint L'Ouverture, who is celebrated throughout the Caribbean, as well as in his native Haiti. Following the slave uprising of 1791 Toussaint led the takeover of the French colony of St Dominigue and successfully repulsed a British invasion from Jamaica. In 1802 Napoleon Bonaparte's soldiers attempted to restore French control over St Domingue. They captured Toussaint and he died in a French prison, but his success as a revolutionary is commemorated in his name L'Ouverture, which means 'the opener'. In 1804 Toussaint's successor Dessalines triumphantly proclaimed the free black republic of Haiti.

▶ Trelawney Town in Jamaica. The Maroons were given the freedom and possession of this land in 1739 provided they did not attack white planters, they gave assistance to the government against external or internal attack and that they returned runaway slaves for a reward.

The indentured workers

After their emancipation many slaves left the plantations to become peasant farmers. This happened particularly in Guyana, Jamaica and Trinidad where there was more free land and where the slaves were encouraged to leave by some Protestant missionaries. However, many slaves stayed on the plantations where they were in a familiar environment and had an assured livelihood. They were now labourers who had to be paid, although the wages were low.

The sugar plantations were in financial trouble for two reasons: they were facing competition from the other colonies and beet sugar was being grown in Europe. In addition their supply of labour was disappearing. To solve this the planters began to import labour under indenture, that is, contract.

Indentured labourers
Europeans, Africans, East Indians and Chinese all went to the Caribbean as indentured labourers. The majority of the Europeans either died or returned home, although a number of Portuguese stayed in Guyana and Scots in Jamaica. The Chinese workers went mostly to Cuba, Guyana, Jamaica and Trinidad.

Amongst indentured workers it was the East Indians who eventually made the greatest impact on the Caribbean. East Indian migration ensured the survival of the sugar industry in Guyana and Trinidad. Work on the plantations was hard and the wages low. Housing and sanitation were poor, disease was rife. The East Indians were protected from beatings and torture, but they were taken to court for trivial offences. There were many riots and strikes in both Guyana and Trinidad.

The labourers were contracted to work for first five years, then ten. At the end of their contract they were guaranteed a free passage home. However they soon realised that conditions in the West Indies were better than many of them had experienced in India and, as they were often given land instead of wages, many decided to stay.

Cultural identity
Unlike the Africans, since they were not slaves, East Indians were permitted to retain their cultural identity. They could speak their own languages, cook their own food, follow their religion – basically Hindu and Islam – and wear their own clothes. The arrival of the indentured workers tended to keep the wages on the plantations low, so there was friction between them and the former slaves, who regarded them as strike breakers. The government made no effort to promote good relations between the Africans, East Indians and other indentured peoples. Such good relations would have been a potential political threat.

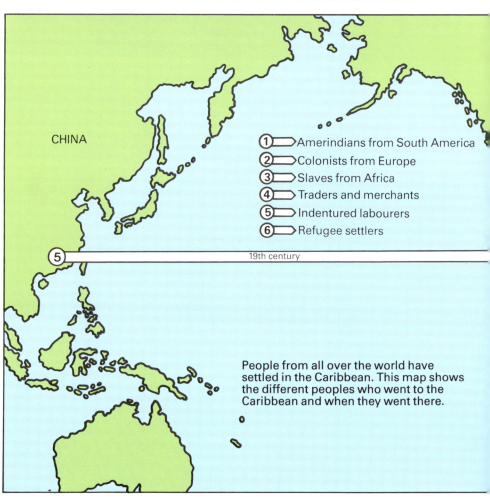

CHINA

① ⟩ Amerindians from South America
② ⟩ Colonists from Europe
③ ⟩ Slaves from Africa
④ ⟩ Traders and merchants
⑤ ⟩ Indentured labourers
⑥ ⟩ Refugee settlers

⑤ ——————————————————— 19th century

People from all over the world have settled in the Caribbean. This map shows the different peoples who went to the Caribbean and when they went there.

▼ A Dougla boy. Dougla is the name given to people of mixed African and East Indian ancestry living in the Caribbean. Although they have a distinctive name the Douglas are well integrated into the multi-cultural society of the Caribbean.

◄ Indentured Indian workers in Trinidad, breaking cocoa pods. Cocoa is a major agricultural crop in the Caribbean. It is the seeds inside the pods that make cocoa, so before mechanisation a large labour force was needed.

▲ A Chinese shopkeeper, whose ancestors were probably indentured labourers about a hundred years ago. Many of the Chinese people who stayed in the area became shopkeepers or opened restaurants.

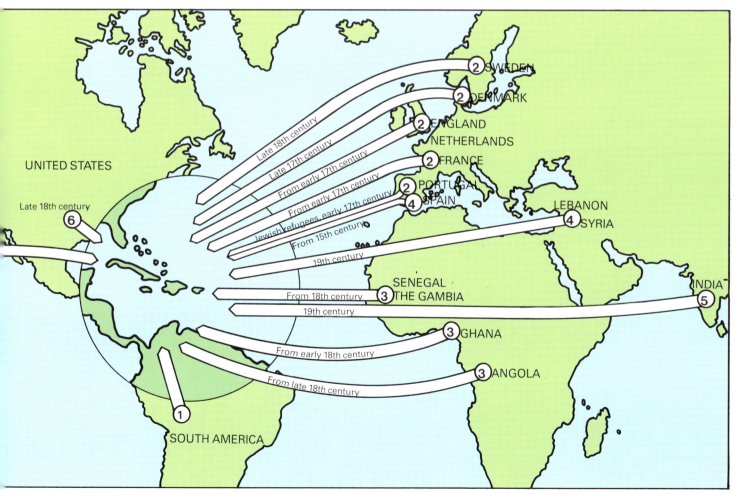

The Caribbean today

▲ The Red House, home of Trinidad's parliament. Today all adults may vote, but in colonial times the parliament only represented the small minority who owned land. Until 1944, 95 per cent of the people of Britain's Caribbean colonies had no vote.

Emancipation gave slaves freedom, but not necessarily justice. They were still subordinate to the landowners. Only those people with a certain amount of land had the vote, and as the former slaves had little or no land, they had no vote.

The Spanish colonies were the first to achieve independence. Haiti was the first Caribbean republic, declared in 1804. The eastern part of Hispaniola became independent of Spain in 1844 as the Dominican Republic. In Cuba and Puerto Rico the settlers joined with the freed slaves to fight for independence, which they gained by the end of the nineteenth century.

Independence
In the English-speaking countries the majority of the people were very poor. There were few trade unions, no political parties and only the landowners had a vote. During the 1930s, strikes and demonstrations for an improved standard of living and political independence began. Marcus Garvey, C. L. R. James, George Padmore and J. J. Thomas were among those who awoke and encouraged black pride. This agitation led to the formation of trades unions and the demand for change in the colonial system of government. It was not until the 1960s that the English-speaking countries were granted independence.

The French-speaking countries of French Guiana, Guadeloupe and Martinique became overseas departments of France in 1946. They send representatives to the French Parliament in the same way as any other part of France, and their citizens are regarded as French. The Dutch-speaking islands have a parliament of their own but remain associated with the Netherlands. Surinam, however, became an independent republic in 1975.

Different situations
Today some Caribbean countries have democratically elected governments, a few have military rulers, but most countries are now independent. There are few links between the countries of different languages, but efforts are being made to change this.

▼ The Caribbean Labour Congress (CLC) held its founding meeting in Barbados in 1945. The CLC was a Caribbean-wide organisation which worked for an independent federation of the colonies. It broke up in the 1950s, but in its short life it had a formidable impact. A number of prominent national figures can be identified here: T.A.Marryshow of Grenada, first president of the CLC (middle row, fifth from right); Grantley Adams, later Prime Minister of Barbados (middle row, fourth from right); Vere Bird, later Prime Minister of Antigua (back row, third from right).

◄ Uriah 'Buzz' Butler was born in 1897 in Grenada. Like many Grenadians he worked in the Trinidad oilfields where he organised strikes and hunger marches. After he was arrested, copies of this photograph were circulated among fellow workers who collected money to help with his defence. Butler was one of the first Trinidadian leaders to unite people of East Indian and African origin. He later became an active parliamentarian and died in 1977.

▼ This diagram shows the structure of the Caribbean Community or Caricom. Caricom was set up in 1973 by the English-speaking countries who wished to form special trade and economic links with each other.

▲ T. A. Marryshow of Grenada was a keen supporter of the idea of a single independent Caribbean-wide state made up of the English-speaking countries.

▼ Luis Muñoz Marin became the first elected governor of Puerto Rico in 1948. He is seen here (right) with President Truman of the United States of America. Marin rejected independence in the hope that American investment would help Puerto Rico to prosper.

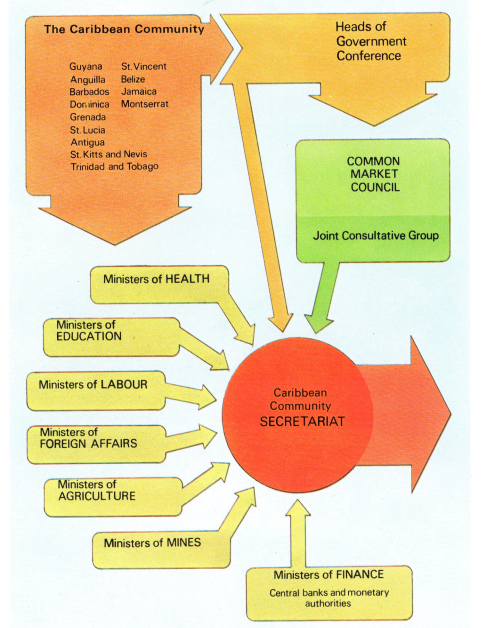

The Caribbean Community

Guyana   St. Vincent
Anguilla   Belize
Barbados   Jamaica
Dominica   Montserrat
Grenada
St. Lucia
Antigua
St. Kitts and Nevis
Trinidad and Tobago

Heads of Government Conference

COMMON MARKET COUNCIL

Joint Consultative Group

Ministers of HEALTH

Ministers of EDUCATION

Ministers of LABOUR

Ministers of FOREIGN AFFAIRS

Ministers of AGRICULTURE

Ministers of MINES

Caribbean Community SECRETARIAT

Ministers of FINANCE
Central banks and monetary authorities

21

A new culture

The Caribbean is an area of cultural diversity and growth. Its culture has evolved through the contributions made by the many different peoples living in the region. Each country has its own cultural identity, but there are common regional themes. Music and dance are the most important artistic forms and the drum is the principal traditional instrument.

The drum is important in both African and East Indian culture. Some fifty years ago a modern version of the drum was created in Trinidad – the steel drum. It is made from discarded steel oil drums whose tops can be shaped to produce a range of notes. The most important festival for steelband players is Trinidad's carnival.

Carnival!

Carnival came to the Caribbean as a Roman Catholic festival before Lent. In Trinidad and Tobago the slaves celebrated the anniversary of their freedom every year. As the government made these celebrations difficult, the Africans joined their festival with carnival. Gradually they took more dominant part in the carnival. Today it is a national festival for everyone. Trinidad and Tobago has the largest and most famous carnival, but it is a festival celebrated throughout the region. Carnival is based on calypso music and dance.

Reggae, which developed in Jamaica, is another new form of music. It is defiant and aggressive, expressing the will of the ordinary Jamaican to resist the pressures of life.

The East Indians kept their traditional music, but in recent years they have merged both western instruments and calypso and jazz into their music.

Dance

Throughout the Caribbean there are similar popular dance patterns whose roots are recognised as distinctly African. There are the Jonkonnu dances of Jamaica and the Bahamas, whose performers wear distinctive costumes to play out set roles. The Dominican Republic holds a special festival for the 'merengue', its most famous dance, while the Cuban rumba is danced worldwide.

Writers of influence

During this century most of the writers of the Caribbean have been concerned with the development of a West Indian personality. They have tried to counter the image of Caribbean people as depicted through the eyes of Europeans. V. S. Naipaul, Nicholas Guillen, Vic Reid, George Lamming, Edgar Mittelholzer and Derek Walcott are all famous Caribbean writers. C. L. R. James, Eric Williams, Franz Fanon and Walter Rodney are thinkers and historians who have added to the understanding of newly independent countries throughout the world.

▲ A scene from the Jamaican film *The Harder they Come*. It tells the story of a country boy who goes to Kingston looking for work and falls into bad company. The film stars Jimmy Cliff who sings several lively reggae songs.

▼ *Fantasy in Realism* by the Haitian painter and sculptor Jasmin Josef. This style of painting is characteristic of Haiti. Although Haiti is one of the poorest countries of the Caribbean it has some of the finest art in the region.

▲ A performance of *The King must Die* by the National Dance Company of Jamaica under the direction of Rex Netleford. Beryl McBurnie of Trinidad and Ivy Baxter of Jamaica are also pioneers of modern dance.

▶ Trinidad's carnival has been acclaimed as one of the world's greatest spectacles. It combines the music and song of steelband and calypso, with the creativity of costume making, that can depict anything from the horrors of nuclear war to the beauty of Tobago's coral reef. For two days before the beginning of Lent in the Christian calendar people parade the streets in costume, dancing to the music of steel and brass bands.

◀ Brother Everard, the versatile Rastafarian artist from Jamaica. He is well known both as the painter of intricate motifs and landscapes and as a maker of unusual musical instruments.

▼ The Mighty Sparrow is the world's most famous calypso singer. The calypso originated in Trinidad, but can be traced back to the songs of the slaves. Calypsos can be serious, political, amusing or satirical.

23

Language and religion

Language and religion were important areas used by the colonisers to impose their culture. Slave owners were always anxious to split up people speaking the same language, so inevitably the African languages disappeared. The loss of language contributed to the loss of identity with Africa.

The history of the Caribbean is reflected in the development of language. Dutch, English, French or Spanish is the official language in each country, but Creole is often spoken by the majority of the people. Creole is a language which combines a European language with the syntax and some words from the west coast of Africa. In French colonies a Creole language evolved which is so stable and identifiable that it is possible for people from Dominica, French Guiana, Haiti and St Lucia to understand the Creole each other speaks. In Curaçao another Creole language called Papiamento has emerged. This is influenced by Spanish because Venezuela dominated Curaçao's market trade. In the islands colonised by the Spanish many Amerindian words have entered the local language.

African religions

The slave owners also did not allow the Africans to practise their own religions. They imposed Christianity, so today the Caribbean is dominated by European forms of religion.

However the African religions often survived by masking the true African ritual beneath Christian practices. Roman Catholicism is the main Christian denomination in the Caribbean. One major surviving African religion is Orisa, the religion of the Yoruba people in Nigeria. In some countries it is known as Shango, the name of one of its main deities; in Cuba and Puerto Rico it is called Lucumi. This religion has survived in a form that is recognisable when it is compared with religion in West Africa today. The Maroons of Jamaica preserved a cult of the Congolese called Myalism, which is related to the voodoo of Haiti.

A wholly new development is the Rastafarian religion in Jamaica. This takes its name from Ras Tafari, that is, Emperor Haile Selassie of Ethopia, whom his followers regard as a deity. Rastafarianism has come to symbolise the rejection of the black people of the Caribbean of all cultural forms from Europe.

East Indian language and religion

Although their languages were not attacked directly in British colonies, the East Indians eventually adopted English as their natural language. Today only a minority can speak an Indian language. However, in Surinam the East Indians, Javanese and Chinese have all retained their languages for everyday use. The Chinese in Guyana, Jamaica and Trinidad have become English speakers.

Hindu and Islam have not just survived but flourished in the Caribbean. Although they have evolved differently from the practice in the Indian continent, the main core remains the same.

▲ Louise Bennett-Coverley is a celebrated Jamaican storyteller, pantomime performer and folklorist. She has written numerous stories in Jamaican Creole. These have encouraged Jamaicans at home and abroad to take a pride in their own language.

▼ Kapo is a self-taught painter and sculptor who has exhibited his work in London and New York. He is the 'shepherd' or leader of a Pocomania community in Jamaica and his work shows religious and African influences. Some of his finest pieces are carved from lignum-vitae wood, obtained from the native guaiacum tree.

▲ A baptism ceremony in the Bahamas. A number of Christian sects have a strong following including the Pentecostalists, Seventh Day Adventists, Jehovah's Witnesses and the African Methodist Episcopal church.

▼ Voodoo comes from Dahomey in Africa, and today is the strongest religion in Haiti. This dancer is 'possessed', she would feel no pain if she were to walk on hot coals, which is meant to indicate the presence of a spirit within her.

▼ The Mikve Israel Synagogue, built in 1732 at Willemstad, Curaçao. Many Jews fled from Spain and Portugal to the Caribbean in the sixteenth century.

▲ A Hindu temple in Trinidad. Hinduism is practised as widely as Christianity in Guyana and Trinidad. This temple is very similar to any that might be found in India.

Famous people

The Caribbean has many heroes, past and present. Stories from long ago have been passed down through generations telling of the valiant defenders of freedom against the invading Europeans, or of brave independence fighters. There are also present-day heroes, men and women, who have become famous both nationally and internationally – politicians, intellectuals, writers, artists, social workers, musicians and sportsmen.

Caonabo

Caonabo is a hero of the past. He was a Carib chief who lived peaceably on Haiti with four Arawak chiefs and their people, when the Spanish landed on the island. The Spaniards changed the island's name to Hispaniola, built a fort called La Navidad and left a few settlers to guard it. When, some time later, the Spanish boats returned the fort had been destroyed. The settlers had gone in search of Carib gold, had fought Caonabo and his warriors and lost. Caonabo united the Caribs and Arawaks against the Spanish, but finally he was tricked, captured and chained aboard a ship bound for Europe. He died at sea in 1494. His fate was similar to that of Toussaint L'Ouverture who died at the hands of the French nearly three hundred years later.

Independence leaders

Frantz Fanon, who lived from 1925 to 1961, was born in Martinique. He became a spokesman for all colonial people through his book *Wretched of the Earth*. His opinions grew out of experience in his home country, medical training in France and work as a psychiatrist in Algeria during the guerilla war against France in the 1950s.

Marcus Garvey became a hero to black people in the Caribbean and beyond. He was born in Jamaica in 1887 and died in England in 1940. He founded the Universal Negro Improvement Association in the United States which aimed to unite black people throughout the world. In 1920 he also founded the Black Star shipping line which was intended to strengthen links with Africa. He never visited the African continent for which he lived, but he influenced both African and black American leaders.

▲ C. L. R. James was born in Trinidad in 1901. He became a distinguished journalist, political thinker and lecturer. He is a central figure in the modern development of black culture. He has lived in the United States and the United Kingdom.

▲ Learie Constantine, as well as being a great cricketing all rounder, was a lawyer, politician, diplomat and campaigner for racial equality. He was a founding member of the Trinidad Nationalist Party and eventually became the first black man to sit in the House of Lords.

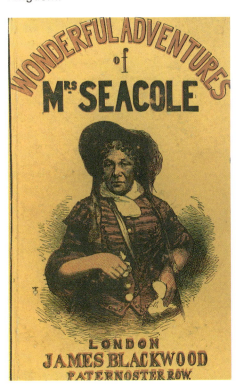

▲ Mary Seacole, half Jamaican and half Scottish, was a formidable humanitarian. She travelled alone to the Crimean War to help care for the soldiers. Every day she would go out looking for wounded and hungry men whom she would nurse and feed.

▲ Hasely Crawford, of Trinidad and Tobago, Olympic gold medallist in 1976. At the same Games Don Quarrie of Jamaica and Alberto Juantorena of Cuba won gold medals.

▲ Fidel Castro, President of Cuba. Castro led the revolution which overthrew the American-backed government of Batista to set up the socialist Republic of Cuba in 1959. Since the Revolution Cubans are healthier, better educated, housed, fed and there is full employment. Cuba has strong links with the Soviet Union.

◄ Bob Marley, Rastafarian and reggae artist who died in 1981. Marley's music did much to spread the Rastafarian religion from Jamaica to the rest of the world. His influence on music and Jamaicans both at home and abroad has been far-reaching.

► Aimé Césaire was born in Martinique. He is one of the most respected literary and political figures in the French-speaking Caribbean. He believes that black people should be aware of themselves as black, and should feel linked to black people all over the world.

27

After sugar

Sugar is still a major part of the economy in many Caribbean countries, but after the abolition of slavery it became important to diversify into other forms of agriculture.

The new crops

In the English-speaking countries, particularly Barbados, Belize, Guyana, Jamaica and St Kitts, the final blow to the plantation system came in 1846 when the British government reduced the price of West Indian sugar exported to Britain. The value of land fell and many estates were abandoned. The freed slaves became peasant farmers and grew a wide variety of crops for selling.

Coffee, tobacco, citrus fruits and bananas became important crops in Jamaica, citrus fruits and bananas became major exports from St Kitts and many of the other Eastern Caribbean islands. Over half the population of St Lucia is employed in the banana industry. Grenada is sometimes known as the Spice Island because of its main agricultural export.

The Bahamas were never prosperous during the sugar period as they were subjected to constant attack by pirates and buccaneers. The cultivation of fruit and vegetables and the fishing of sponges and seafood are now all flourishing exports.

Salt and aloes

In the Dutch-speaking countries of St Eustatius, Saba, St Maarten and Bonaire, salt and aloes are the main agricultural exports. Rice was introduced into Surinam and grown by the Javanese and East Indian workforce; it has now become the country's principal export crop. Rice is also a major export crop of Guyana.

Access to Europe

The position of French Guiana, Guadeloupe and Martinique differs from that of the other Caribbean countries. Their status is similar to the mainland of France, so their crops and other goods for export have ready access to the European Economic Community. They also import many European goods. Much of the land of Guadeloupe and Martinique was traditionally devoted to the production of sugar and bananas. However, the increasing production of beet sugar in France has led to the closure of most of the sugar plantations in Martinique.

Fishing and coconuts

Cuba's economy is centred around sugar, but its tobacco industry is very strong and its fishing industry is fast growing. Puerto Rico has only produced sugar since the abolition of slavery. It is now the largest exporter of fresh coconuts to the United States, in addition to being a major exporter of citrus fruits.

▲ The cropping of the sugar harvest is now mechanised. This machine does in a few hours what took many slaves many days. Mechanical sugar-cane cutters, like this one in Guadeloupe, make the production of sugar more profitable.

◀ Arrowroot fields in St Vincent, with an old processing factory in the background. St Vincent is one of the world's leading producers of arrowroot, which is one of the island's most important exports. The thick underground stem of arrowroot is the source of a particularly pure form of starch used for medicinal purposes.

▲ The salt pans on Anguilla are separated from the sea by a narrow spit of sand. Salt is obtained from sea water by evaporation and is one of the few natural resources of this tiny island. Salt was one of the region's major attractions to the European explorers.

▲ Packing bananas in Martinique. Bananas can bruise and deteriorate rapidly, so careful packing and refrigeration in transit are essential. The banana tree can grow to six metres or more. The trunk of the 'tree' is made of the stems of the huge banana leaves. Bananas are the second largest crop export from the Caribbean after sugar.

▼ Curing tobacco in Cuba. Cuba is famous for its quality tobacco, its hand-rolled Havana cigars are possibly the best in the world. Tobacco is a native crop to Cuba.

▼ Coconuts are grown commercially throughout the Caribbean and form the basis of a number of industries. The oil is used for cooking and making soap. Coir fibre, which comes from the husk, is used for matting and as a filling for mattresses. The nut itself provides milk and the soft white flesh is used in cooking.

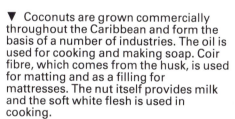

Industry and technology

The development of the many natural resources of the Caribbean has been the basis of its industry. The most important of these is oil. Oil was discovered in Trinidad and has provided the island with a source of wealth and employment ever since. Fifty years after its discovery, two-thirds of the country's exports are oil-related. Trinidad has a large petro-chemical complex, making it one of the most industrialised countries in the Caribbean.

Bauxite is another important natural resource for heavy industry. It is mined principally in Jamaica, Guyana and Surinam, but also in Haiti and the Dominican Republic. Jamaica is the second largest producer of bauxite and alumina in the world. It supplies the United States with much of its requirements. The price of bauxite has fallen recently which has affected the economies of those countries which depend on its export.

Tourism is a major industry both in large countries like Jamaica and small ones like Antigua. Tourism is subject to outside influences, such as changes in the economies of the richer countries, and inside ones, like domestic political unrest.

New industries

Over the past few decades many governments have encouraged the development of manufacturing industries, so as to diversify from agriculture and to reduce the dependence on exports. Both these problems were the legacy of colonial government. Many items that were imported are now made in the larger countries, like Barbados, Cuba, Guyana, Jamaica and Trinidad and Tobago. Assembly factories, especially of electronic goods, which need cheap skilled labour, are being established in a number of Caribbean countries.

Developing technology

Science and technology have played an important part in the development of the Caribbean. The

▲ The Kirkvine works near Mandeville, Jamaica, where bauxite is converted to alumina in the first stage in the production of aluminium.

Caribbean Industrial Research Institute (CARIRI) was established in 1970. Its purpose is to develop expertise and research which governments and small industries cannot afford to implement. It aims to encourage businesses to invest in the development of local expertise before investing in imported technology. It also advises on the adaptation of imported technology to local conditions, and on the updating of imported technology. The Institute has, for example, developed a rice thresher for use in small and medium farms.

▼ The oil refinery at Willemstad, Curaçao is operated by the Shell company which is based in Europe. It was opened in 1918 to refine oil produced in Venezuela. In 1929 an American-owned refinery was opened in Aruba. The refineries have been a major source of employment in Aruba, Curaçao, Bonaire, and have attracted people from Grenada, St Kitts, Saba, St Maarten and St Eustatius.

▲ Dockers on the way to work at Bridgetown, Barbados. Good port facilities are essential for trade between the islands and further afield. The deep-water harbour at Bridgetown was opened in 1961. Ports are now being modernised to deal with container traffic.

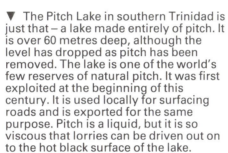

▼ The Pitch Lake in southern Trinidad is just that – a lake made entirely of pitch. It is over 60 metres deep, although the level has dropped as pitch has been removed. The lake is one of the world's few reserves of natural pitch. It was first exploited at the beginning of this century. It is used locally for surfacing roads and is exported for the same purpose. Pitch is a liquid, but it is so viscous that lorries can be driven out on to the hot black surface of the lake.

▲ An assistant performing routine analysis at the Windward Islands Banana Association (WINBAN) laboratories. An epidemic plant disease can blight an entire island and set its economy back for years.

31

Family life

There is no single lifestyle which is characteristic of the whole Caribbean area. Even though many are small islands, within a single country there may be tremendous differences, especially between town and country.

A mother's society

The experience of slavery has left its mark on the family life of the Afro-Caribbean. From the beginning of slavery to emancipation the African man in the Caribbean was often only marginally responsible for his family. Since all slaves were the property of the master, the male slave could neither protect nor provide for his family. Children born on the estate belonged to the master. Marriage was not recognised, nor were stable relationships encouraged. It has not been easy to counter the effects of this, so that many Afro-Caribbean families today are matrifocal. Caribbean women are noted for being self-reliant and for successfully bringing up their children on their own. There are many families in which the household is headed by the mother and maternal grandmother. The extended family, which includes other relations, is still a very tightly-knit group. Since the 1960s, an additional problem is that fathers must often live away from their children where they can find work. Recently women have had to travel away from home in the search for work.

East Indian men were not separated from their families when they were indentured workers. The East Indians were also allowed to keep their religion and other cultural forms and values, which helped preserve much of their family structure and lifestyle. The extended family is still a very strong feature of their culture, as is their community sense.

Community responsibilities

There is a great sense of community in Caribbean life, especially in the rural areas. People greet each other easily and neighbours traditionally feel a responsibility for the children and elders among them. Most West Indian parents, African and East Indian alike, bring up their children very strictly. Both communities set great store by respect for elders and also insist that their children receive a good education.

The different people who make up the cosmopolitan Caribbean community live together in harmony. In the countries with a significant Indo-Caribbean population, it is usually the East Indians who still work on the sugar estates or in agriculture, as the Africans have moved towards urban life. However these divisions are in no way rigid and East Indians can also be found in every profession and non-agricultural job.

Houses and homes

The influence of a Caribbean country's history can be seen in its buildings. Euro-American styles are the most common, but there are Indian influences and remnants of African ideas. Structures are adapted according to local building materials and local weather conditions. In some countries it is, for example, important that buildings should be able to withstand the high winds of hurricanes. The homes being built today tend more and more to be blocks of flats or housing developments to meet the ever increasing demand for housing in the cities.

▲ A Hindu wedding in the Caribbean. Family life for the East Indians in the community is much the same as in India. At the same time the East Indians have integrated with the Africans who were living in the Caribbean before they arrived as indentured workers.

▼ A middle-class family at home. The family is very important in the Caribbean. At the weekend or on public holidays relations gather to spend time together, probably with grandmother at the centre.

▲ Life on the verandah in Port Antonio, Jamaica. The verandah is a traditional feature in many parts of the Caribbean and is ideal for the tropical climate. It provides shelter from the sun and rain and catches any breeze.

▼ Modern flats on the outskirts of Havana in Cuba. Housing development is proceeding fast, but even so it is difficult in many countries of the Caribbean to keep pace with the need for new housing in the cities.

▼ A small farmstead in St Vincent. Many of the small farms set up after the liberation of the slaves still exist as family plots, growing food for the family and for sale at the local market.

Food and eating

As with many aspects of Caribbean life, the food is mixed and varied. The Arawaks and Caribs cultivated fruit and vegetables such as sweet potatoes, cassava, pineapple and coconuts. The slaves were not able to bring their traditional foods from Africa, but were able to retain their styles of cooking, curing and preserving. The East Indian and Chinese indentured workers introduced rice, spices, new fruits and vegetables, as well as new methods of cooking. In addition the European settlers added their influence to the cooking of particular countries. Caribbean cooking has developed from the various influences of its many peoples.

No meal is dull with the many local herbs and spices which are available. Nutmeg, annatto, pimento, mace, parsley and thyme all add their special flavours. The many varieties of burning hot chillis are an essential ingredient of several dishes, while ginger, lime juice and coconut also add their characteristic flavour.

Beans and vegetables are a major part of the Caribbean diet. Gungo or pigeon peas are a rich source of protein, as are red beans, split peas and black-eyed beans. Carrots, tomatoes, pumpkin and okra are all popular vegetables. In a dish of African origin, meat is added to a bean-and-vegetable dish after it has been browned in sugar and hot oil. This would then be eaten with either rice, yam, dasheen, plantains, green figs, sweet potatoes or cassava. This main meal is usually eaten at midday, although for many families it may be the evening as city habits spread.

Curries, eaten with rice or roti, are standard fare for East Indians, but they have also been adopted as a national dish and are cooked nutritiously by all ethnic groups.

Variety of names
The variety of names for food can be confusing. Callaloo is a favourite dish in Guadeloupe, Trinidad and Guyana. It is made with the leaves of the dasheen plant, boiled with okra, pumpkin, onions, cooking butter, coconut and seasoning. 'Bakes' are popular throughout the Caribbean, but in Jamaica they are called Johnny cakes or fried dumplings. There are plain or coconut roast bakes and fried bakes, eaten for breakfast instead of bread. Coconut milk, used in coconut bakes, is a favourite ingredient in Caribbean cooking. Coocoo, the national dish of Barbados, is also of African origin. Different versions of it can be found in other islands, such as Curaçao. Chinese cooking is exceptionally popular, as is shown by the large number of Chinese restaurants, but it is also popularly cooked at home by many West Indian families.

The Caribbean has fruit in abundance. Fine weather all the year round guarantees a constant supply of a variety of fruits. Some fruits are exported, like citrus fruits, bananas, avocadoes and mangoes; but there are many others that do not travel so easily, among them pawpaws, sapodillas, soursop, pomeracs and pomme cythères.

▲ An open air market in Haiti. The smallholders sell their produce here and are able to buy from other traders to meet their own needs.

▼ A market stall at Port Antonio in Jamaica carrying a range of local fruit. The Jamaican government provides transport for fresh farm produce from local depots to its own shops. The system guarantees the farmer a fair price and encourages production.

▲ Supermarkets are taking over from
traditional shops, especially in the cities.
Large supermarkets are being built in
every town, particularly on the outskirts
to cater for car owners.

▲ A section of the famous floating
market at Willemstad, Curaçao. Local
fishermen sail up to the road and sell
their catch without leaving their boat.
Fruit and vegetables are also sold there.

▼ A selection of some of the fruit,
vegetables, beans and spices grown in
the Caribbean. Plantains and pawpaw,
ackee and okra, sweet potatoes and yam
are among this array of produce.

Education for all

Education in the Caribbean tends to reflect the culture of the European country which colonised each particular country. None of the European colonisers provided education for the slaves. They did not think it necessary for slaves to be educated and were worried that education might stir up unrest. All Caribbean countries now regard education as a vital part of their political and economic development.

Church schools

In some countries it was the churches that provided a basic education. After emancipation the British government granted money to the Protestant churches to provide teachers and buildings for the schools. It was through the church schools, both Protestant and Roman Catholic, that an education system began to emerge. Even so the town schools tended to have more than their fair share of resources, leaving many rural schools with poor buildings and few teachers. These schools provided a basic education, but education was not compulsory and many people were illiterate.

It was not until recently that primary education became compulsory. In most English-speaking countries a lack of money has meant that the schools run a shift system, some children going to school in the mornings, others in the afternoon.

French-speaking schools

The curriculum for schools in French Guiana, Guadeloupe, Haiti and Martinique is French-based. When Haiti declared itself a republic in 1804, there was not a single school in the country. One of the aims of the revolution was to provide education for all, but the cost of war and the levy of payment for property seized from the British and French, made this impossible. Even today there is still great poverty and a high rate of illiteracy in Haiti. Most schools are run by the Roman Catholic church. In French Guiana, Guadeloupe and Martinique the school system is more widespread than in Haiti. Students still travel to France for higher education, but there is a university in the islands.

Although Puerto Rico is a dependency of the United States its culture is basically Spanish. The United States tried to impose English as the main language in schools, but the Puerto Ricans resisted this and Spanish is still their main language in schools.

Radio and television

The media is a major source of education. Both radio and television are used for education at many different levels. Local newspapers are important for those adults who have just learned to read, encouraging them to read and educate themselves further. The French- and Dutch-speaking islands have the widest variety of newspapers.

▲ A class in one of Jamaica's basic schools, which prepare children for primary school. The government provides teachers and pays the running costs, but each community has to provide the buildings. Jamaica's education policy guarantees education for everyone up to seventeen years of age.

▲ Students at a St Vincent secondary school studying chemistry. In the English-speaking countries education followed the British pattern. Until recently the exam syllabuses were set in Britain, but since 1979 the Caribbean Examination Council has provided its own syllabus and exams to meet local needs.

▲ These primary-school children in Belize reflect the multi-racial society of the Caribbean. The children are descended from the different peoples of the Caribbean, who came from Africa, Europe and India. Children at English-speaking schools often wear a uniform of a white shirt and with a coloured scarf.

▲ An adult literacy class in Cuba. Many of today's adults had only a very poor or even no school education. The revolution in 1959 set itself the goal of making all Cubans literate. In 1961 a mass adult education programme was launched and over three-quarters of a million adults were taught to read and write.

◄ H.M. Queen Elizabeth presenting degrees at the Trinidad campus of the University of the West Indies. The University, which has three campuses, was founded in 1948. Some of the faculties include law, medicine, agriculture, engineering, arts and humanities. The University is a strong influence linking the English-speaking countries of the region.

► The first newspaper in the English-speaking Caribbean was the weekly *Jamaica Current* which began publication in 1718. Bermuda's *Royal Gazette*, founded in 1828, is the oldest surviving title. The press and broadcasting play an important part in supplementing formal adult education.

Sport and leisure

As in most countries sport is important for both competition and pleasure. The Caribbean has a fine record of achievement in the Olympic Games and competition within the region always runs high during the Central American and Caribbean Games. The region is particularly successful at athletics and boxing. Cycling, an old established sport, takes place on the road in Caribbean-wide meets.

Cricket

In the English-speaking countries cricket is the most popular game. It was introduced from England in 1850 and rapidly caught on at all levels of society. Even so, it was not until the 1960s that fully integrated teams based on merit were chosen for international competitions. During the annual Cup Match in Bermuda there is even a two-day public holiday. At all matches the spectators are well informed and passions run very high. In recent years the West Indies team have emerged as world champions.

Ball games

In Puerto Rico archaeologists have uncovered the site of a playing field which shows that ball games have been played in the Caribbean since the days of the Arawaks. Today netball, baseball, basketball, softball, volley ball and football continue the tradition.

The sea

The many beaches and islands of the Caribbean are popular for a day out on Sundays and public holidays. Surfing, swimming, water skiing and boating are enjoyed by many people. During the years of slavery there was very little leisure. The African slaves were not allowed to celebrate their traditional festivals, but holidays were sometimes granted to keep Christian festivals like Christmas and Easter. Today public holidays vary from country to country. For some the anniversary of independence is a holiday; for others

the date of the emancipation of the slaves. In Trinidad and Guyana, Hindu and Moslem religious festivals, as well as Christian, are national holidays. In the countries which celebrate carnival the preparation normally lasts around two months. It is a time enjoyed by everyone, with parties, visits to the calypso tents, the steelband yards and the special carnival shows.

▲ Football is popular throughout the Caribbean. Local competitions are organised between amateur teams and there are inter-country tournaments.

▼ Cricket is not just a sport to watch but a game to be played. The West Indies has produced a number of outstanding players in recent years. These include Gary Sobers, Clive Lloyd, Viv Richards and Michael Holding. Barbados is well known for providing many talented players.

▲ Playing netball at the Jamaican school named after the athlete Don Quarrie. Women's netball teams are of a very high standard. The Trinidad and Tobago women's national team has been Commonwealth champion.

▼ A domino match in progress. Dominoes is taken very seriously and generates great excitement among players and spectators. In many public squares in the cities there are special facilities for playing the game.

▲ The cinema is a great attraction for many people, but its popularity is lessening in some countries with the arrival of home videos. This small local cinema in Haiti still manages to draw the crowds to its doors.

▲ Playing the pans. 'Pans' are made from old oil drums. Different sized depressions are made in the top of the drum with skilful use of hammer, chisel, oil and fire. Each depression will be tuned to sound a different note when beaten with a wooden stick.

Transport and communication

Good communications are essential to link the countries of the Caribbean. The six Dutch-speaking countries, for example, are separated by 1500km. Internal travel is usually by road. The roads are being improved all the time, but the general standard tends to be inadequate. Buses are a common means of transport, but the number of cars is always increasing, with the resulting problems of traffic.

Only a few of the bigger countries like Cuba and Jamaica have rail networks. In many countries it is the problem of the terrain, which is not suitable for railway lines.

Many islands now have their own airports with inter-Caribbean and international flights. Air transport is tending to replace sea travel, but ships still play an important part in the transport of freight.

Radio and telephone communications are far in advance of other forms of local communications and form an important link between the widespread countries of the Caribbean.

Barbados
Independent (1966)
Capital: Bridgetown
Area: 430 sq.km
Population: 252,000
Language: English

Belize
Independent (1981)
Capital: Belmopan
Area: 23,000 sq.km
Population: 160,000
Languages: English, Spanish

Bermuda
British dependent territory
Capital: Hamilton
Area: 55 sq.km
Population: 55,000
Language: English

Cuba
Independent (1901)
Capital: Havana
Area: 117,000 sq.km
Population: 10,000,000
Language: Spanish

Curaçao (Netherland Antilles)
Netherlands dependent territory
Capital: Willemstad
Area: 330 sq.km
Population: 165,000
Languages: Dutch,
Papiamento, Spanish, English

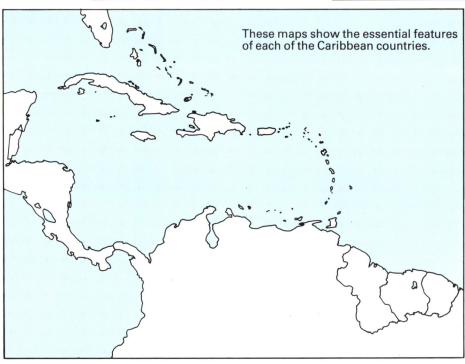

These maps show the essential features of each of the Caribbean countries.

Anguilla
British dependent territory
Capital: Valley
Area: 155 sq.km
Population: 7,000
Language: English

Antigua and Barbuda
Independent (1981)
Capital: St John's
Area: 440 sq.km
Population: 79,000
Languages: English

Aruba
Netherlands dependent territory
Capital: Oranjestad
Area: 190 sq.km
Population: 67,000
Languages: Dutch,
Papiamento, Spanish, English

Bahamas
Independent (1973)
Capital: Nassau
Area: 13.800 sq.km
Population: 270,000
Language: English

Bonaire (Netherland Antilles)
Netherlands dependent territory
Capital: Kralenijk
Area: 288 sq.km
Population: 10,000
Languages: Dutch,
Papiamento, Spanish, English

British Virgin Islands
British dependent territory
Capital: Road Town
Area: 130 sq.km
Population: 12,000
Language: English

Cayman Islands
British dependent territory
Capital: Georgetown
Area: 260 sq.km
Population: 18,000
Language: English

Dominica
Independent (1978)
Capital: Roseau
Area: 750 sq.km
Population: 75,000
Languages: English, Creole

Dominican Republic
Independent (1844)
Capital: Santo Domingo
Area: 48,500 sq.km
Population: 6,600,000
Languages: Spanish, various
Creoles

French Guiana
French overseas department
Capital: Cayenne
Area: 83,500 sq.km
Population: 73,000
Language: French

Grenada
Independent (1974)
Capital: St George's
Area: 345 sq.km
Population: 88,000
Languages: English, Creole

Guadeloupe
French overseas department
Capital: Basse Terre
Area: 17,000 sq.km
Population: 330,000
Languages: French, Creole

Guyana
Independent (1966)
Capital: Georgetown
Area: 215,000 sq.km
Population: 950,000
Language: English

Haiti
Independent (1804)
Capital: Port-au-Prince
Area: 27,750 sq.km
Population: 5,270,000
Language: French, Creole

Jamaica
Independent (1962)
Capital: Kingston
Area: 11,400 sq.km
Population: 2,300,000
Languages: English, Creole

Martinique
French overseas department
Capital: Fort de France
Area: 1,100 sq.km
Population: 325,000
Languages: French, Creole

United States Virgin Islands
US dependent territory
Capital: Charlotte Amalie
Area: 350 sq.km
Population: 100,000
Language: English, Creole

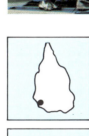

◄ Loading bananas on to a banana boat in St Lucia. The fast refrigerated vessels run by the banana companies are an essential link between the Caribbean plantations and their big markets in Europe and North America.

Montserrat
British dependent territory
Capital: Plymouth
Area: 100,000 sq.km
Population: 12,000
Language: English

Puerto Rico
Associated with United States
Capital: San Juan
Area: 8,900 sq.km
Population: 3,197,000
Languages: Spanish, English

Saba (Netherlands Antilles)
Netherlands dependent territory
Capital: Bottom
Area: 13 sq.km
Population: 1,000
Languages: Dutch, English

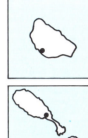

St Eustatius (Netherlands Antilles)
Netherlands dependent territory
Capital: Oranjestad
Area: 21 sq.km
Population: 1,300
Languages: Dutch, Papiamento, Spanish, English

St Kitts-Nevis
Independent (1983)
Capital: Basseterre
Area: 260 sq.km
Population: 44,500
Language: English

St Lucia
Independent (1979)
Capital: Castries
Area: 620 sq.km
Population: 45,000
Languages: English, Creole

St Maarten (Netherlands Antilles)
Netherlands dependent territory
Capital: Philipsburg
Area: 34 sq.km
Population: 16,000
Languages: Dutch, English

St Vincent & the Grenadines
Independent (1979)
Capital: Kingstown
Area: 390 sq.km
Population: 128,000
Language: English

Surinam
Independent (1975)
Capital: Paramaribo
Area: 164,000 sq.km
Population: 370,000
Languages: Dutch, Hindi, Javanese, Creole

Trinidad & Tobago
Independent (1962)
Capital: Port of Spain
Area: 5,000 sq.km
Population: 1,160,000
Languages: English, Creole

Turks & Caicos Islands
British dependent territory
Capital: Grand Turk
Area: 430 sq.km
Population: 7,500
Language: English

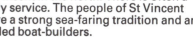

◄ Some of the schooners which make regular trips linking the Grenadines with St Vincent in the north. There is often a daily service. The people of St Vincent have a strong sea-faring tradition and are skilled boat-builders.

A brief history of the Caribbean

THE AMERINDIAN PERIOD
Communal homes built in western Caribbean. Cultivation of tobacco, sweet potato and cassava on a large scale. Skills in pottery, weaving, canoe-building and canoeing.

SPANISH COLONISATION
1492 Spanish expedition led by Christopher Columbus lands in Bahamas.
1494 Spanish colony of Santo Domingo founded on Hispaniola.
1508–11 Spanish begin to settle in Puerto Rico, Jamaica and Cuba.
1510 First West Africans arrive as Spanish slaves.
1515 City of Havana, Cuba, founded by Spain.
1527 Black slaves revolt in Puerto Rico.
1538 University founded in Santo Domingo.
1540 English and French pirates start to raid Spanish ships and ports in the Caribbean.

THE STRUGGLE FOR LAND
1585 Francis Drake leads English raiding expedition which destroys the town of Santo Domingo.
1624 British colonies established on St Kitts and Barbados, French colony established on St Kitts.
1630–40 Dutch seize Curaçao, Saba, St Maarten and St Eustatius.
1635 French settle Guadeloupe and Martinique. Compagnie des Isles d'Amerique set up to administer French settlements.
1640–50 Dutch, French and British start to grow sugar, ending the Spanish monopoly. Land values rise steeply – up to 30 times in under ten years.
1641 Caribs drive off British forces trying to invade St Lucia.
1655 Britain captures Jamaica from Spain.
1665 Western part of Hispaniola taken over by France as the colony of St Domingue.
1671 Denmark acquires the Virgin Islands.
1688 Death of Henry Morgan, one of the last of the British pirates.

1697 Treaty of Ryswyck signed, in which Spain formally recognised St Domingue, and putting an end to piracy by the French.
1739 War in Jamaica between escaped slaves (Maroons) and the authorities.
1783 Britain defeated in American War of Independence. British refugees from America flee to the Bahamas with their slaves.
1797 Britain takes over Trinidad from Spain.

REBELLION AND NATIONALISM
1804 Slaves in St Domingue revolt. They defeat the French and set up the republic of Haiti.
1807 Britain stops trading in slaves.
1815 France formally recognises British rule in Grenada, Dominica, St Vincent, Trinidad and Tobago.
1833–8 Slavery abolished in British colonies and replaced by a system of apprenticeship.
1834 Rebellion against apprentice-ship system in St Kitts.
1836 A railway is completed in Cuba – the first in Latin-America.
1844 Eastern part of Hispaniola becomes independent as the Dominican Republic.
1848 Slavery abolished in the French colonies.
1851 Cuba stops trading in slaves.
1861 Dominican Republic brought under Spanish rule following repeated invasion by Haitian troops.
1865 Rebellion put down at Morant Bay, Jamaica. Dominican Republic finally becomes independent.
1866 Oil discovered in Trinidad.
1868 War of independence begins in Cuba.
1874 Truce declared in Cuban war.
1886 Slavery finally abolished in Cuba.
1898 United States occupies Puerto Rico during Spanish-American war.
1899 United States takes over administration of Cuba.
1902 Cuba becomes independent. St Pierre, Martinique, is destroyed when Mt Pelée erupts, killing 40,000 people.
1917 United States buys Virgin Islands from Denmark.
1922 Imperial College of Tropical Agriculture founded in Trinidad.
1942 Large bauxite reserves confirmed in Jamaica.
1944 All adults in Jamaica get the right to vote.

1946 French Guiana, Guadeloupe and Martinique become *départements* of France.
1952 Puerto Rico becomes an autonomous commonwealth within the United States.
1958 British colonies are combined to form the West Indies Federation.
1959 Fidel Castro leads victory parade into Havana.

INDEPENDENCE AND DEVELOPMENT
1961 West Indies Federation breaks up.
1962 Jamaica becomes independent, followed by Trinidad and Tobago.
1966 Barbados and Guyana become independent.
1973 The Bahamas become independent.
1974 Grenada becomes independent.
1975 Surinam becomes independent.
1978 Dominica becomes independent.
1979 St Lucia and St Vincent and the Grenadines become independent.
1981 Antigua, Barbuda and Belize become independent.
1983 St Kitts-Nevis becomes independent.

Index

GULF OF MEXICO

Sarasota
Fort Pierce
U.S.A.
L. Okeechobee
Fort Myers
West Palm Beach
The Everglades
Fort Lauderdale
Everglades
Miami
C. Sable
Florida Bay
Key West
Florida Keys
Straits of Florida

85
80
75

Grand Bahama I.
Little Abaco I.
Freeport
Great Abaco. I.
Bimini Is.
New Providence I.
NASSAU
Eleuthera I.
BAHAMAS
Andros Town
Andros Island
Cat I.
San Salvador
Great Exuma
Long I.
Jumento Cays
Crooked I.
Acklins I.

25

Tropic of Cancer

HAVANA
Guanabacoa
Marianao
Matanzas
Cárdenas
Canal Nicolas
Guanajay
Javellanos
Sagua la Grande
San Antonio de los Banos
Güines
Colón
Pinar del Rio
Batabano
C
Santa Clara
Caibarién
Canal Viejo de Bahama
Guane
Guane
Cienfuegos
Placetas
U
Morón
Cayo Romano
C. San Antonio
Nueva Gerona
Trinidad
Ciego de Avila
B
Nuevitas
Yucatan Channel
I. de la Juventud
Arch. de los Canarreos
Sancti Spiritus
Florida
Puerto Padre
Gibara
Great Inagua
C. Catoche
Camagüey
A
Banes
Tizimin
Victoria de las Tunas
Holguin
Antilla
Valladolid
Cozumel
Jardines de la Reina
Bayamo
Palma Soriano
Baracoa
Cozumel I.
G
Manzanillo
Windward Passage
20
C. Cruz
Sierra
Maestra
MEXICO
Little Cayman
Cayman Brac
2000
Santiago de Cuba
Guantánamo
R
Chetumal
Grand Cayman
Cayman Trough
−7680
E
Jérémie
Montego Bay
Falmouth
St. Ann's Bay
A
Belize City
Negril Point
JAMAICA
Port Antonio
Les Cayes
Turneffe Is
Savanna la Mar
Morant Point
BELIZE
May Pen
Spanish Town
KINGSTON
T
Gulf of Honduras
I. de la Bahia
Swan Is.
E
Puerto Cortés
C. Camaron
R
C A R I B B
Tela
La Ceiba
San Pedro Sula
HONDURAS
Caratasca Lagoon
15
C. Gracios a Dios
Coco
Colombian Basin
San Miguel
Tegucigalpa
Cayos Miskitos
Choluteca
Puerto Cabezas
Cord. Isabella
Esteli
Jinotega
Chinandega
Matagalpa
Tuma
I. de Providencia (Col.)
Corinto
León
NICARAGUA
I. de San Andres (Col.)
MANAGUA
Masaya
Bluefields
Islas de Maiz
Diriamba
Granada
Jinotepe
El Bluff
Lago de Nicaragua
Rivas
Santa Marta
Cienaga
Sa. Nevac de San M
5800
San Juan del Norte
Barranquilla
Sabanalarga
Fundación
10
COSTA
Puntarenas
Alajuela
Cartagena
Arjona
Calamar
RICA
SAN JOSÉ
Cartago
Limón
Cord da Talamanca
Pta Manzanillo
COLOMBIA
Puerto Quepos
Bocas del Toro
CANAL ZONE
Colón
Lorica
Sincelejo
Magangué
3374
Almirante
Chepo
Sincé
Mompos
El Banco
Golfito
BALBOA
PANAMA
G. of Darien
Montería
Sinú

West from Greenwich 85
80
75